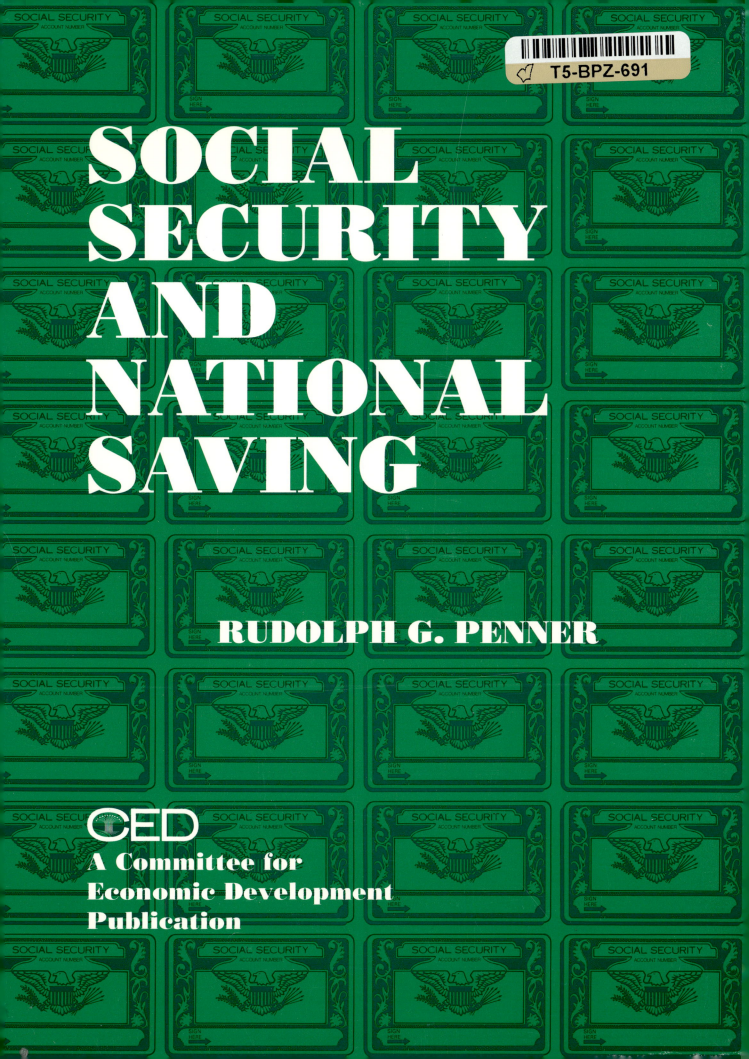

SOCIAL SECURITY AND NATIONAL SAVING

RUDOLPH G. PENNER

CED

A Committee for
Economic Development
Publication

The Committee for Economic Development is an independent research and educational organization of over two hundred business leaders and educators. CED is nonprofit, nonpartisan, and nonpolitical and is supported by contributions from business, foundations, and individuals. Its objective is to promote stable growth with rising living standards and increasing opportunities for all.

All CED policy recommendations must be approved by the Research and Policy Committee, a group of sixty trustees, which alone can speak for the organization. In addition to statements on national policy, CED often publishes background papers deemed worthy of wider circulation because of their contribution to the understanding of a public problem. This paper has been approved for publication as supplementary paper number 249 by an editorial board of trustees and advisors. It also has been read by members of the Research Advisory Board, who have the right to submit individual memoranda of comment for publication.

While publication of this supplementary paper is authorized by CED's bylaws, its contents, except as noted above, have not been approved, disapproved, or acted upon by the Committee for Economic Development, the Board of Trustees, the Research and Policy Committee, the Research Advisory Board, the research staff, or any member or advisor of any board or committee, or any officer at CED.

Library of Congress Cataloging-in-Publication Data

Penner, Rudolph Gerhard, 1936-
        Social security and national saving.

            Includes bibliographies references.
1. Social security—United States.
2. Saving and Investment—United States.
3. Retirement income—United States.
I. Title.
HD7125.P387 1989   368.4'301'0973   89-9779
ISBN 0-87186-249-2

Price: $7.50
Committee for Economic Development
477 Madison Avenue, New York, NY 10022/(212) 688-2063
1700 K Street, N.W., Washington, D.C. 20006/(202) 296-5860

SOCIAL SECURITY AND NATIONAL SAVING

Rudolph G. Penner

A Committee for Economic Development Publication

CONTENTS

FOREWORD

By Robert C. Holland
President, Committee for Economic Development

The hundreds of billions of dollars that pour into and out of the Social Security System each year have enormous economic as well as social effects on our nation. What happens to those billions of dollars over the next few years and into the next century is of critical concern to all Americans.

Social Security and National Saving, while reflecting the views of CED advisor Rudy Penner, Senior Fellow at The Urban Institute, continues and reinforces CED's long-standing concern for ensuring a sound future for Social Security.

In 1981, CED issued Reforming Retirement Policies which warned that a retirement disaster was on the way and called for a combination of public and private actions to increase pensions and saving and reform Social Security.

This statement made an important contribution to retirement policy reforms in the early 1980s. The study offered a number of proposals to avert the then-looming insolvency of the Social Security Trust Fund, including changes in tax treatment, a reduction in benefit increases, and a gradual increase in the retirement age. A number of these proposals were subsequently enacted.

These recommendations were again reinforced in 1984 with the publication of Social Security: From Crisis to Crisis? which warned that changes made to the system in 1983 provided a very small margin of safety. The statement called on Congress to develop additional measures to ensure Social Security's solvency.

Again in 1988, in Investing in America's Future, we stressed the role of a healthy Social Security system in a strong and competitive economy. This statement argued that unless certain adjustments are made, current Social Security surpluses "may not be sufficient to avoid real hardships and insecurity for future retirees and inequitable burdens on future working generations... Consequently, the government should strongly consider policies to increase national saving."

Marshaling the political will to make choices now to avoid harder choices later is never an easy task. I believe that this paper will make an important contribution to helping the Congress, the Administration, and the public reach some important conclusions on issues that we avoid at our peril.

We are deeply grateful to Rudy Penner for the insight and intellect he brought to this project. We also wish to thank Roy L. Ash, chairman of the CED Task Force on Social Security, and the advisors to the Task Force (listed on page vi) for their comments on Dr. Penner's successive drafts. Recognition is also due to William J. Beeman, CED's vice president and director of macroeconomic studies, who served as staff counsellor to the project and guided it through the CED process.

v

TASK FORCE ON SOCIAL SECURITY

vi

ACKNOWLEDGMENTS

I wish to thank the CED Task Force on Social Security, particularly its chairman Roy Ash, for providing thoughtful comments on the earlier drafts of this paper. Special thanks are also due to Henry J. Aaron and Robert J. Myers for providing extensive comments on the paper and valued advice on several technical issues. My appreciation is extended also to Barbara Willard for providing the secretarial support for this paper.

The comments received improved the paper in many respects. Nevertheless, disagreements remain on the issues discussed in this paper and I am solely responsible for the analysis and recommendations in this paper.

Rudolph G. Penner
Senior Fellow
The Urban Institute

INTRODUCTION

The nation is about to experience a dramatic demographic change. The rate of growth of the population age 65 and over, which rose 2.4 percent a year in the period from 1950 to 1985, will slow dramatically to 1.2 percent annually between 1985 and 2005 because of the birth trough during the Great Depression. After 2005, the baby boomers of the 1940s and 1950s will reach retirement age, and the over-65 population will again grow at 2.4 percent annually between 2005 and 2025.

Although this is the same rate of growth experienced for the elderly population over the past thirty-five years, the labor force will be growing slowly because of the rapid decline in the birth rate since the late 1950s. As a result, the ratio of the working-age population to the elderly will fall steadily except for a brief respite between 1995 and 2005. In 1950, there were 7.2 people age 20 to 64 for each person 65 and over. By 1985, the ratio had fallen to 5.0; and by 2025, it will be 2.9 under the demographic assumptions favored by most students of the Social Security system. The ratio will continue to fall until it reaches 2.6 in 2035 and then will decline more slowly to 2.4 in 2060.

Obviously, those working after the first decade of the twenty-first century will face a growing burden as they attempt to fulfill the promises made to the retired when the burden was not so large. More than half of the nondefense, noninterest outlays of the federal government go to the elderly. The largest program by far involves the payment of Social Security benefits. The second most impor-

tant program is the rapidly growing Medicare system. Housing subsidies and nutritional assistance, though much smaller, also go disporportionately to the elderly. Therefore, the fiscal burden to be faced by future workers will extend far beyond Social Security unless current policies are altered significantly.

The key policy question raised by the demographic swing is: Should we help future workers cope with the coming burden, and if so, how? Whether or not we should help depends on a political value judgment. We cannot help without imposing costs on ourselves, and the question is whether it is worth it to make our children and grandchildren better off. This analysis will not debate that issue; it will take as a given that we should be more sympathetic, than we have been recently, to the plight of our descendants as they face the growing burden of supporting the elderly in the twenty-first century.

If that judgment is accepted, the question becomes: How should we help? The most straightforward approach is to raise national saving. This will increase national wealth either by slowing the rate at which we are accumulating liabilities abroad or by raising our own real capital stock. To the extent the latter occurs, future productivity and wages will rise and workers will be better able to afford the benefits promised to the elderly.

The most direct approach to raising national saving is to reduce the federal budget deficit. The slow growth in the elderly population through 2005 will ease spending pressures and give us a golden opportunity to be more prudent fiscally.

The huge budget deficits of recent years would be of little concern if private saving had risen to compensate. Unfortunately, private net saving relative to net national product was lower in 1987 than at any time over the past three decades and seems to have been on a strong downward trend since 1984. The combination of this problem and future demographic trends makes budget deficit reduction much more urgent.

Chart 1 illustrates the course of net national and net private saving since 1960. Net national saving is net private saving less government dissaving. Therefore, the difference between the net national and net private saving lines indicates the extent to which the federal budget deficit has drawn on net private saving. For the purposes of the chart, the surpluses of state and local government have been included in private saving. State and local surpluses have been on a strong upward trend since 1960 because of the need to finance their employees' pension funds. Personal and business saving has been on an even steeper downward trend than Chart 1 suggests.

Recent gross private saving has behaved better than net saving, the difference being the depreciation of the nation's capital stock. Because depreciation may be overstated, some economists argue that gross saving provides a better indication of the degree to which the nation is preparing for the future. Further, as depreciated investment is replaced,

the average quality or technical sophistication of the capital stock is improved.

I shall not comment on the merits of such arguments here because they are not especially reassuring. Private gross saving averaged 16.6 percent of gross national product (GNP) in the 1960s and 18.6 percent in the 1970s. In the 1980-1987 period, the average fell slightly to 18.2 percent; but like net private saving, gross private saving has been declining rapidly since 1984. Clearly, there is nothing in this record that warrants running a federal budget deficit in the 1980s averaging to 4.1 percent of the GNP. The deficit has lowered the total national saving rate significantly below the level of the previous two decades while the demographic outlook argues the need for more saving, not less.

Although the basic issue goes far beyond Social Security, the reduction in demographic pressures through 2005 will allow the Old-Age, Survivors, and Disability Insurance (OASDI) trust funds to accumulate large surpluses. The OASDI annual surplus is now included in the federal budget deficit that is targeted in the budget process. It is used to finance a part of the non-OASDI deficit and therefore masks the extent to which non-OASDI expenditures are out-running non-OASDI revenues.

A RECENT HISTORY OF SOCIAL SECURITY POLICY

Legally, OASDI has been run on a partial-reserve basis. Over the past thirty years, this has practically implied that it operated, until recently, as a pay-as-you-go system. Operationally, this implied an attempt,

CHART 1

NET NATIONAL AND NET PRIVATE SAVING
As a Percentage of Net National Product, 1960 to 1987

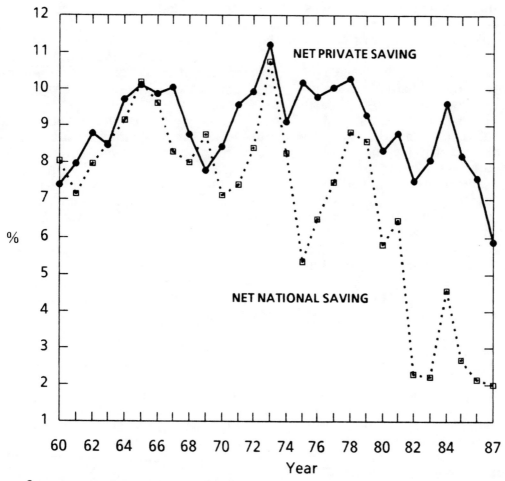

NET PRIVATE SAVING

NET NATIONAL SAVING

%

Year

Source: U. S. Department of Commerce, <u>Survey of Current Business</u>, various issues.

4

on average, approximately to equate payroll tax revenues to benefit outlays seventy-five years into the future.

The system has a trust fund into which annual surpluses are deposited and from which deficits are subtracted. The fund is invested in U.S. Treasury securities. It was never envisioned that the fund would contain sufficient resources to finance its future obligations in full. Since the early 1960s, the reserve is best understood as a cushion to cover brief periods when the system's cash flow was negative, say because of a recession. Munnell and Blais have estimated that a fund equal to 85 percent of outlays is adequate to cover most contingencies and that a fund equal to 145 percent of outlays would cover all but the worst of economic catastrophes.[1] A target equal to one year's outlays is probably a reasonable goal if all that is desired is to provide an adequate cushion against almost all contingencies.

Prior to 1972, Social Security benefits were not explicitly indexed. Whether or not the system was in actuarial balance was calculated using extremely conservative economic assumptions. As the economy performed better than was assumed, annual surpluses grew, and benefits were adjusted upward or broadened periodically by explicit acts of Congress.

The unusually rapid growth of the economy in the 1960s led Congress to believe that it could be much more generous toward the elderly, and it rapidly raised benefits in the late 1960s and early 1970s. Accelerating inflation also implied that

benefits had to be adjusted periodically so that beneficiaries would not suffer unduly from an erosion in their purchasing power.

But Congress began to worry about whether such increases could be provided in a disciplined manner. It was concerned that every time an adjustment had to be made, strong political pressures would push it into being overly generous. The increases of the late 1960s and early 1970s exceeded not only the inflation rate but also the rate of growth of wages.

Congress therefore decided to automate the system so that explicit benefit adjustments would be required less frequently. Benefits and the wage base of the payroll tax were both indexed in 1972. The indexing system used for benefits was designed to provide increases slightly in excess of inflation so that, with real wage growth, the elderly's earnings replacement rate, as computed at age 62, would remain roughly constant as the economy grew.

The indexing system would have worked well if wages had increased at about 4 percent per year and inflation had been half that rate; but as inflation accelerated, the new system meant that real benefits grew ever more rapidly. This was misleadingly referred to as double indexing, and it clearly had to be corrected.

The indexing system was adjusted in 1977. The benefits received by the elderly were linked to the Consumer Price Index (CPI) as they had been before, and the formula that determined initial benefits was largely indexed to wages. The goal of the new system was to keep the real value of the benefits of retirees, as determined at age 62, growing along with the covered wages of workers.

Unfortunately, the economic assumptions used to plan the financing of the system proved far too optimistic. Moreover, the CPI used at the time to index benefits overstated the inflation rate because it greatly exaggerated increases in the cost of housing.

As a result, the OASDI trust funds were depleted. By 1981, they had fallen to less than 20 percent of benefit outlays. They soon would not have been sufficient to cover even small irregularities in the cash flow of the system throughout the year, and there was a danger that the system would become technically bankrupt.

A commission, under the chairmanship of Alan Greenspan, was appointed to recommend solutions to the problem. Most of the commission's recommendations were adopted by Congress, which also decided to increase the age at which full benefits were paid from 65 to 67 beginning gradually early in the twenty-first century.

It was the primary goal of the reforms, enacted in 1983, to solve the short-run financing problem while moving the system toward actuarial balance for the next seventy-five years. Payroll taxes were increased, a portion of benefits was subjected to income taxation, and along with the change in the normal retirement age, other less important adjustments were made to benefits. But given the relatively slow growth in the elderly population early in the seventy-five-year period and the more rapid growth thereafter, the reforms implied, as a by-product, that the trust funds would

initially build up a very large surplus that would be depleted later.

The economic and demographic assumptions used by the commission were fairly conservative, and the trust fund has now begun to build up reserves. The annual excess of receipts over outlays reached about $40 billion in 1988, and trust fund resources are now sufficient to cover more than 40 percent of outlays. These surpluses will eventually reach gargantuan levels. The annual surplus will peak at over $400 billion in the second decade of the twenty-first century and the trust fund will contain almost $12 trillion, or the equivalent of about 25 percent of the GNP in 2030. Relative to outlays, the accumulated reserve will peak at 531 percent in 2015. But it is not really a surplus because it is not sufficient to cover future obligations. After 2030, the trust fund will be quickly depleted if policies are not changed, and it will be exhausted shortly before 2050 (see Table 1).

This analysis will analyze policy options for responding to the immense growth and rapid depletion of the trust fund. But, first, it is useful to explore the reliability of the assumptions underlying the projections. The accumulated trust fund balances still amount to less than one year's outlays, and the bitter experiences of the late 1970s and early 1980s teach us that Murphy's law is alive and well and that it is important to guard against overoptimism.

WILL THE SURPLUS ACTUALLY MATERIALIZE?

The OASDI annual surplus is the difference between two larger numbers, income and outlays. A given

Table 1

Estimated Operations of OASDI Under the IIB Assumptions,

Calendar Years 1988 to 2045

(In billions of dollars)

YEAR	TOTAL INCOME	TOTAL OUTLAYS	ANNUAL SURPLUSES	ASSETS AT END OF YEAR
1988	262.7	222.4	40.3	109.1
1990	309.5	252.2	57.3	211.9
1995	447.9	338.3	109.6	645.5
2000	631.5	446.8	184.7	1,409.4
2005	886.3	595.1	291.2	2,632.5
2010	1,237.9	825.8	412.1	4,460.6
2015	1,686.3	1,203.7	482.6	6,763.0
2020	2,226.2	1,775.4·	450.8	9,124.3
2025	2,857.0	2,549.4	307.6	10,996.2
2030	3,590.7	3,524.5	66.2	11,837.5
2035	4,452.6	4,703.2	(250.6)	11,240.0
2040	5,470.6	6,121.7	(651.1)	8,840.4
2045	6,674.3	7,966.8	(1,292.5)	3,799.4

Source: 1988 Annual Report of the Federal Old-Age and Survivors Insurance and Disability Insurance Trust Funds (Washington, D.C.: U. S. Government Printing Office,1988) p. 131.

percentage change in income or outlays, therefore, results in a larger percentage change in the surplus. The annual surplus is, in turn, invested in Treasury securities which pay interest that is compounded over time. The projected accumulated surplus in the trust fund is thus very sensitive to relatively small changes in payroll tax receipts, benefit outlays, and the assumed interest rate earned on the trust fund balance.

Because projections are so sensitive to economic and demographic assumptions, the OASDI trustees provide four sets of projections based on combinations of assumptions ranging from optimistic to pessimistic. They also provide estimates of the effects of changing only one variable on the actuarial balance of the system. Actuarial balance is defined as the difference between the present value of future benefits and income both divided by the present value of the payroll tax base.

Real Wage Growth

The growth of real wages in the economy will depend crucially on the rate of growth of labor productivity, which, in turn, will be determined by the rate of capital formation, the pace of technological change, and the quality of the labor force as it is affected by education, training, and experience. All these variables can be affected to some degree by changes in public policy, and indeed, much of this analysis involves policy decisions that may be important to national saving and the pace of capital formation. In other words, the rate of increase of real wages is not entirely determined from the outside, although exogenous factors will affect it. It will also be controlled to some degree by the

choices of policy makers and by which of the options discussed in this analysis are eventually adopted. A more rapid growth in real wages raises the real value of payroll tax revenues through time and therefore improves the outlook for the trust fund. In the longer run, it also raises the real value of benefits because the initial computation of benefits is influenced by past real wages. But this operates with a time lag, and once someone retires, benefits are held constant in real terms. Consequently, a more rapid rate of growth of real wages has a net beneficial effect on the actuarial balance of the system.

The intermediate IIB projections of the trustees, which will be used for most of this analysis, assume that the annual rate of growth of real wages rises to 1.7 percent by 1992 and then falls to 1.4 percent by 2000. It stays at this level for the remainder of the projection period.

This rate is considerably lower than the 2 percent annual growth of the 1960s but represents a significant improvement over the experience in the 1970-1986 period, during which real wages grew less than 0.5 percent per year. The reasons for the abrupt fall in productivity growth are not well understood, although the fact that the labor force became younger and the nation experienced two energy crises during the 1970s and two recessions in the early 1980s probably played a role in the dismal performance. Other factors have been studied, but no one has been able to explain the change fully.[2]

Without a complete explanation of the slowdown, it is extremely difficult to speculate about the future. The IIB assumptions imply that a large part of the decline was temporary, and this may be somewhat optimistic. That is, it may take extremely wise national policies to attain a rate of real wage increase as high as 1.4 percent in the long run. But our lack of knowledge of the causes of the decline obviously hampers our ability to design such policies.

The optimistic assumptions of the trustees (Alternative I) project a 2.4 percent rate of increase in the long run, a higher rate than was experienced in the ebullient 1960s. This is probably far more optimistic than can be achieved even with the best policies.

The pessimistic assumptions (Alternative III) project a 0.9 percent annual rate, which is higher than the experience of the past ten years. Thus, the whole range used by the trustees may be somewhat optimistic.

If the assumed rate of wage growth is lowered by 0.5 percentage points while all other IIB assumptions are retained, the actuarial balance of the system for the next seventy-five years is worsened by about 0.5 percent of payroll. In other words, it would take a 0.5 percentage point increase in the payroll tax rate to compensate for this deficiency.

Inflation

Even though the Social Security system is fully indexed, an increase in the inflation rate slightly improves its actuarial balance, because higher inflation is assumed to affect payroll tax revenues immediately while benefit increases lag about one year. The IIB assumptions project a 4 percent inflation rate in the long run, whereas the optimistic assump-

tions project 2 percent and the pessimistic assumptions 5 percent. Thus, an optimistic assumption for the economy is a pessimistic assumption from the point of view of the financial health of the system, and vice versa. A 1-percentage-point increase in the inflation rate improves the actuarial balance of the system by 0.20 percent of the tax base.

A 4 percent inflation rate is far higher than that experienced for most of the nation's economic history and was considered to be intolerable for the long run twenty years ago. But expectations have changed as a result of double-digit inflation in the 1970s and early 1980s, and now 4 percent seems quite acceptable. Whether it will remain so for seventy-five years is another question; with a 4 percent rate, prices double every eighteen years. Nevertheless, increased tolerance for inflation seems destined to remain with us for a long time, even if not for the entire seventy-five years, and the assumption is not unreasonable.

Real Interest Rates

The IIB assumptions project a real interest rate of 2 percent. This is far lower than the 5 to 6 percent averaged thus far in the 1980s but higher than rates experienced in the 1970s, when real rates were negative in some years. A lower real interest rate diminishes the earnings of the trust fund. But it does not have much effect on the income rate used to compute the actuarial balance because future income, though higher, is discounted more heavily. The cost rate is diminished because the high costs of the twenty-first century are also discounted more heavily. A 0.5-

percentage-point increase in the real interest rate results in a net improvement in the actuarial balance equal to 0.24 percent of payroll.

Whether or not the large decline in real interest rates implied by the IIB assumptions is realistic depends crucially on national saving policy in the long run. If saving can be increased, rates of return on capital will be reduced and the assumption is reasonable. Again, an assumption that is optimistic for the economy is pessimistic for the trust fund. The trustees use a higher real rate of 3.0 percent in their optimistic assumptions and a lower real rate of 1.5 percent in their pessimistic assumptions.

Fertility Rates

The fertility rate--that is, the average number of children who would be born to a woman surviving to the end of her childbearing years--has varied widely over recent decades. It reached 3.61 in 1960 and fell to 1.74 in 1976. The IIB assumptions use a rate of 1.9 beginning in 2010, compared with an actual rate of 1.87 in 1987. The optimistic assumptions use a long-term rate of 2.2; the pessimistic assumptions use 1.6. A reduction of 0.3 in the rate implies a worsening of the actuarial balance of 0.49 percent of payroll.

Although the fertility rate is mainly determined by sociological factors, it probably can be influenced in a minor way by public policy. Child-care programs, education costs, the tax system, and other programs are likely to have some influence on the rate in the long run. The IIB assumptions are hard to dispute, but

demographic projections are notoriously unreliable.

Other Assumptions

Many other assumptions are necessary to make a Social Security projection. Death rates, immigration rates, and disability experience all affect the trust funds significantly. Such assumptions will not be discussed here, but all add elements of uncertainty to the projections.

Clearly, the uncertainties are such that it is unwise to accept any specific Social Security projection with great confidence. Nevertheless, there is a high probability that the range of assumptions used by the Social Security actuaries will bracket actual experience. The optimistic assumptions seem too good to be believed, and the pessimistic assumptions, though less extreme, are likely to be improved unless the economy suffers extremely serious problems.

The middle-of-the-road IIB assumptions will be used as a basis for all of the analysis that follows. In my judgment--and any judgment must be put forward with extreme caution--they may be slightly optimistic on balance, but not enough to destroy the relevance of the analysis. The IIA assumptions have not been discussed in detail; they use the same demographic assumptions as the IIB projections and very slightly more optimistic economic assumptions.

The implications of the four sets of assumptions for the ratio of the trust fund balance to annual outlays are shown in Chart 2. The IIB assumptions show the fund peaking at slightly more than five times annual

10

CHART 2

ESTIMATED CONTINGENCY FUND RATIOS, FOR OASI AND DI
TRUST FUNDS COMBINED, CALENDAR YEARS 1987 to 2065

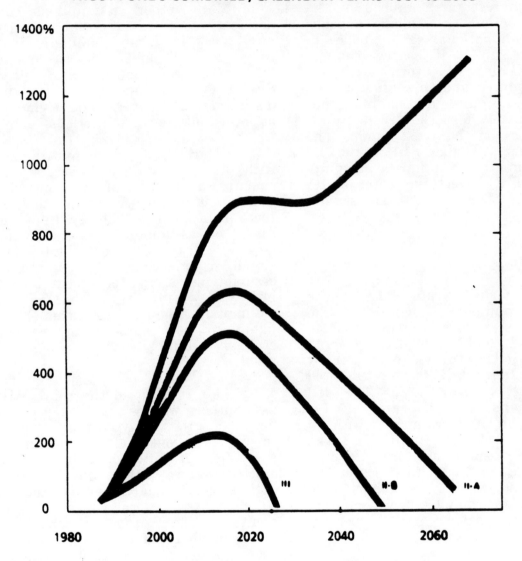

Source: 1988 Annual Report of the Board of Trustees of
          the Federal Old-Age and Survivors Insurance
          and Disability Trust Funds, p.85.

outlays around 2015 and then going broke shortly before 2050. The optimistic assumptions imply that the contingency ratio never declines significantly, and in the unlikely event that the future unfolds in this manner, scheduled payroll taxes would clearly be excessive. At the other extreme, the pessimistic assumptions imply that the fund never exceeds 2.5 times outlays and that it goes broke before 2030.

OASDI AND NATIONAL SAVINGS

As noted earlier, the overall deficit of the federal government plays an important role in determining the national saving rate. Since fiscal 1976, an annual deficit target has been set by a budget resolution, and that target is defined to include the OASDI annual surplus. Gramm-Rudman-Hollings (GRH), passed in late 1985, sets a more rigid set of deficit targets five years into the future. Again, the targets set include the OASDI annual surplus. If the targets are not achieved (within $10 billion) by explicit Congressional action, they are enforced by an automatic spending cut.

The projected growth in the OASDI annual surplus was not explicitly discussed when the GRH targets were set initially and was discussed very little when the targets were amended in 1987. However, the projected OASDI surpluses undoubtedly allowed Congress to set lower targets than would have been possible if the surpluses did not exist. But the targets were probably not lowered by the full amount of the OASDI annual surpluses, since, in their absence, I believe that Congress would have cut non-OASDI spending and raised non-OASDI taxes a bit more vigorously.

Once the targets are set, surprising increases in the annual OASDI surplus probably do not lead to a lower deficit or increased national saving. The GRH deficit target has become a floor as well as a ceiling, so that surprise increases in the OASDI surplus simply provide the wherewithal to increase non-OASDI spending or lower other taxes.

There is a sense in which lending to the rest of government by the Social Security trust fund can be considered an artificial accounting transfer. One can imagine running Social Security without a trust fund. Payroll taxes could be considered part of general revenues, and benefits could be paid out of total revenues without regard to their source. This change would have no economic meaning. If the change did not alter the payroll tax or benefit provisions in current law, the overall deficit of the government would be the same as it is now and its negative impact on national saving would not change.

The change would, however, have considerable symbolic significance. The dedication of payroll taxes to trust funds gives the impression that workers are paying for future benefits and therefore makes workers more willing to pay those taxes.

Although the taxes paid by current retirees and by employers on their behalf in the past fell far short of what would have been required to finance current benefits, this is not widely understood, and many retirees feel that they have property rights to the benefits. This makes it politically difficult to cut those benefits. Moreover, the benefits are not means-tested, and the elderly do not feel that they are dependent on welfare. This also increases political support for the program. In addition,

12

the trust fund balance earns interest paid by the rest of government and, the payroll tax levels required to fund benefits are lower than they would have to be in a system that simply conveyed the payroll taxes of workers to retirees.

Consequently, the symbolism inherent in the artificial accounting techniques used by the Social Security system has undoubtedly had a profound effect on Social Security policy since the invention of the system. It has therefore had important economic effects in the long run, even though it has no immediate economic effects for a given payroll tax and benefit structure.

Any attempt to reduce the total budget deficit faces formidable political obstacles. The contentious struggles of the past few years amply illustrate that point. The difficulty is easy to understand. It is fun to live on borrowed money, especially when the government can borrow on citizens' behalf at lower interest rates than they would pay if they borrowed privately. Whereas the pleasures of borrowing are immediate, the benefits resulting from additional savings take a very long time to accrue.

Although budget deficits are high by historical standards, they are still small relative to the nation's huge stock of physical capital. Therefore, deficit reduction results in only a small addition to the rate of growth of capital even if it is assumed that each dollar of deficit reduction adds a dollar to investment and that this is the most that can be hoped for in the long run. Thus, the effect on worker productivity, wages, and future living standards also proceeds very slowly.

In contrast, the pain caused by program cuts or tax increases occurs immediately. In a typical model of economic growth, it takes twenty-five to thirty years to recoup the initial loss.[3]

If it is assumed that some of the national savings released by deficit reduction reduces capital inflows from abroad, the beneficial effects on domestic capital formation and wages are even smaller. However, a reduced capital inflow allows domestic investors to earn a higher rate of return than they would if all the increased savings were devoted to increased capital formation in the United States.

Although the rate of return on deficit reduction is relatively small, it compounds over time, and the effect on the living standards of our children and grandchildren can be substantial. There are also large long-term effects on the size of the American economy relative to the size of other economies, and therefore, deficit reduction has the potential to affect America's relative military power significantly and our influence in bargaining with other countries over international economic policy.

There are also some short-run effects. The problems created by our large budget deficits have been mitigated by an increase in net capital inflows from abroad that occurred just as our budget deficit soared. (Some would say that the growing budget deficit caused the capital inflow, but this is a controversial interpretation. Moreover, the nature of the causal relationships is not important to this argument.) The inflows of international capital eased the pressure on domestic capital markets, lowered U.S.

interest rates, and helped to maintain a relatively high rate of capital formation.

If failure to reduce the budget deficit reduces the confidence of foreign investors in the future of the U.S. economy and they lower their investment greatly or actually withdraw capital, interest rates could rise significantly. If this process occurred quickly, it would be hard for the United States to adjust and there could be a recession and, in the worst case, a financial crisis. The risk of such a trauma is fairly low, but budget-deficit reduction would decrease it further.

The main reasons for budget-deficit reduction are to make future generations better off and to be better equipped to deal with the large growth in the retired population in the twenty-first century. In other words, to make a strong case for deficit reduction, one must appeal to public altruism, and that is never easy.

The situation is even more complicated than I have indicated so far. To the extent that budget-deficit reduction is successful in increasing the pace of domestic capital formation and future wages, workers will earn higher absolute Social Security benefits in the long run because eventual benefits are so strongly influenced by the wage histories of workers. Consequently, the absolute burden imposed by the retired population in the twenty-first century will be increased although it will be lower relative to total payroll. But the increased rate of capital formation will lower rates of return to capital and indirectly lower interest rates. The earnings of the trust fund on its investment will be reduced, and a higher proportion of future benefits will have to be financed by payroll taxes. However, this last point pertains only to the health of the Social Security system viewed in isolation. Presuming that the system continues to invest in government bonds, a lower interest rate reduces the interest obligations of the rest of government and overall, taxpayers will be better off because of their higher wages and higher capital income.

To the extent that lower budget deficits reduce capital inflows from abroad, wages grow more slowly, the rate of return on domestic capital is not lowered as much, and the absolute burden imposed by future benefits is decreased. The growing integration of world capital markets obviously has an important impact on the distributional effects of deficit reduction. A reduced capital inflow lowers both the wages of workers and their future retirement benefits while it raises the rate of return to domestic owners of capital. It also reduces the drain on future living standards caused by interest and dividend payments to nonresidents.

QUANTITATIVE DIMENSIONS OF THE PROBLEM

This analysis thus far has examined only the qualitative nature of the problem posed by the demographic changes that will be experienced in the twenty-first century. It has not been very precise about the severity of the burden to be faced by future workers. Is that a problem which will cause a crisis, or will it be fairly easy to handle?

The OASDI problem, viewed in isolation, does not appear very serious using the standards favored by most economists. That is to say, the increased burden on future workers is relatively small compared with the size of the GNP or total wages implied by the IIB assumptions for the middle of the next century.

Aaron, Bosworth, and Burtless[4] have computed the payroll tax rate necessary to keep the OASDI system in continuous actuarial balance through 2060, given current benefit provisions. The payroll tax rate implied for 2060 is 14.7 percent, compared with the 12.4 percent scheduled by current law. Even if such a rate increase occurred in one year (and that is not contemplated), and if it is assumed that workers bear the burden of both the employer and the employee share of the tax, workers would regain their pretax increase level of after-tax wages within one year after the tax increase goes into effect, assuming the 1.4 percent annual rate of real wage increases used for the long run by the IIB assumptions.

The same authors have examined changes in national saving policy and their effect on the eventual OASDI burden. In one analysis, the non-OASDI part of government is assumed to keep its deficit equal to 1.5 percent of GNP while the OASDI annual surplus (assuming the system is kept in actuarial balance) is used to reduce the government's overall deficit and eventually to convert it into a surplus. Comparing this option with a base line in which the overall government deficit is held to 1.5 percent of GNP so that increases and then decreases in the annual OASDI surplus have no effect on national saving, the authors show that the increases in the capital stock and worker productivity allow the higher OASDI burden to be absorbed while still increasing society's consumption levels as a share of net national product (NNP) after

2010. This analysis assumes that all extra savings are invested at home.

When the extra savings are invested abroad, the results depend crucially on the rate of return assumed on foreign investments, and the analysis is too complex to be described in detail here. Domestic investors gain by being able to invest abroad, but domestic workers receive no increase in wages or eventual OASDI benefits because domestic capital formation and worker productivity are not affected. The burden of OASDI falls relative to NNP compared with a base line computed under these assumptions because less income has to be transferred abroad. It is difficult, however, to say what happens to consumption. Nevertheless, the burden is unlikely to be severe even if all of the extra savings flow abroad.

The impact of future demographic changes becomes much more severe when the implications of current Medicare laws are considered. Medicare costs rise both because of the growing eligible population and because the costs of medical care are increasing relative to the costs of other goods and services.

To keep the OASDI and hospital insurance (HI) systems in continuous actuarial balance will require a combined OASDI and HI tax rate of slightly above 22 percent in 2060 compared with a scheduled rate of 15.3 percent. If the increase occurred in one year, it would take a worker almost six years to regain the pretax increase level of after-tax real income assuming real wage growth of 1.4 percent per year. Of course, the increase would be phased in gradually, thus allowing fairly steady increases in after-tax income. Nevertheless, the increased burden is substantial. Even if the annual surpluses of the actuarially balanced OASDI-HI system are added to national saving, the burden imposed by OASDI-HI relative with NNP would grow slightly after 2030 compared with the current burden.

When the burden of the non-HI part of Medicare and other spending programs for the elderly is added, the total burden on society grows further, but it can be handled. Consumption may fall relative to NNP as the burden of supporting the elderly rises, but the NNP is so much larger under the IIB assumptions that future workers will have significantly higher living standards than are enjoyed today. That is to say, the nation will have the economic resources to handle the problem, but it may be another question whether the problem can be easily handled politically.

The current difficulty in reducing the budget deficit rapidly is indicative of extreme public hostility to even relatively minor spending cuts or tax increases. Moving to an overall government surplus in the early twenty-first century will take more political courage than has recently been manifested.

A minority of economists believe that the growing OASDI annual surpluses will cure the federal deficit problem and, by implication, the national saving problem without the need to take any heroic fiscal actions. This position may rest in part on a value judgment (not explicitly stated) that the current generation is not obligated to save quite as much as implied by the options I have discussed. But I believe that there is also a tendency to understate the seriousness of the deficit problem in

the non-OASDI operations of the government.

This last point is difficult to prove because official projections of the implications of current law for non-OASDI operations extend only five years into the future and it is difficult to estimate the state of the non-OASDI budget early in the twenty-first century, when the annual surpluses of OASDI will be peaking relative to GNP. However, the five-year projections shown in Table 2 give us some hints regarding the dynamics of the situation in the longer run, and they are disturbing.

The non-OASDI deficit rises over time absolutely, although the implied deficit-GNP ratio does decline slightly. Furthermore, the $40 billion rise in the rest of government's deficit between 1988 and 1994 is almost matched by a $35 billion rise in interest payments from the rest of government to OASDI. This simply reflects the rapid growth in the amounts projected to be borrowed from OASDI by the rest of government. Moreover, the growth in the interest earned by the OASDI trust funds accounts for almost half of the growth in their annual surpluses over the period. Thus, a major contributor to the growth in the annual OASDI surplus, namely interest (and the relative importance of its contribution will grow through time), is also a major contributor to the growth in the rest of government's deficit under current law.

The dynamic implications of current law might best be understood by eliminating interest payments from both the rest of government's deficit and the OASDI annual surplus because the interest payment simply goes from one government pocket to another and

TABLE 2

The OASDI Suplus and the Rest of Government's Deficit, Fiscal Years, 1988 to 1994
(in billions of dollars)

	1988	1989	1990	1991	1992	1993	1994
OASDI Surplus	39	52	63	74	86	99	113
Rest of Government Deficit	194	199	199	206	212	220	234
Interest Received by OASDI	7	11	16	21	28	34	42

Note: The economic assumptions used in this table differ slightly from the IIB assumptions of the OASDI trustees.

Source: Congressional Budget Office, The Economic and Budget Outlook; An Update, (Washington, D.C.: U.S. Government Printing Office, August 1988) pp. 62 to 63.

does not affect the projection of the overall deficit. If the absolute size of the rest of government's deficit without this interest payment remained constant at its 1994 level of $192 billion (probably a somewhat optimistic estimate), it would amount to 1.4 percent of projected GNP in 2005. It is in that year that the noninterest OASDI annual surplus peaks at 1.1 percent of GNP; thus, the overall budget would still not be balanced. Moreover, this calculation implies that there would be little increase in the real value of discretionary non-OASDI spending for almost twenty years. Obviously, it is highly unlikely that OASDI annual surpluses will overwhelm the rest of government's deficits unless some dramatic deficit-reducing actions are undertaken.

Of course, if the OASDI annual surplus were lower during the projection period and no other laws were changed, the rest of government would have to borrow more from the public; and in that sense, the OASDI annual surplus will certainly help lower the overall deficit and reduce the drain on national savings. Another way of indicating the seriousness of the deficit in the rest of government is to note that the total amount of borrowing it has to do from the public and OASDI indicated by the projections of Table 2 implies that its total debt will be growing slightly faster than GNP and its interest bill will be growing faster than its tax revenues well into the 1990s. This clearly makes it somewhat more difficult to get the situation under control without significant spending cuts or tax increases.

The rest of this analysis will explore options for exploiting the existence of the OASDI annual

surplus to add to national saving and to reduce the future burdens imposed by the OASDI and HI systems.

POLICY OPTIONS

There are many options for reducing the overall budget deficit and increasing private saving. This study examines only those that are fairly closely related to the emergence of the OASDI surplus. Options will be evaluated according to their effects on the well-being of different generations of workers and retirees over time and their implications for the distribution of income between workers and retirees within particular time periods.

One obvious option that I will not analyze in detail would be to allow an increased flow of immigration into the United States. This could significantly raise the ratio of workers to the retired population in the twenty-first century. Because recent immigrants tend to have higher birth rates than native-born Americans, it also implies a significant change in the cultural and language composition of the population. In deciding on immigration policy, the nation will have to assess the difficulties, if any, of socially and economically integrating new groups into the population and compare them with the obvious benefits that an increased flow of immigrants would bring.

Changes in Deficit Targeting Procedures

Aaron, Bosworth, and Burtless analyzed the implications of one particular path of increased saving for the burden imposed by OASDI in the future. Current workers would be expected to sacrifice consumption either by accepting immediate cuts in non-OASDI programs or by paying higher taxes. Future workers would then have more wealth and capital with which to improve their standard of living while still supporting a growing retired population. The benefits of future retirees would also be increased to the extent that the increased savings were invested at home and raised lifetime wages.

The implications of other paths for lower deficits or increased saving could be evaluated. For example, the overall deficit path implied by the GRH targets could be accepted through 1993 and an overall surplus equal to, say, 1 percent of the GNP could be pursued thereafter. There is, in other words, no particular reason that the path of increased saving should be related closely to the path of annual OASDI surpluses, although that option gives a particularly appealing result. But the choice of paths is ultimately a value judgment regarding how much should be sacrificed now in order to benefit future generations. As the recent presidential election campaign demonstrated, however, there is a strong propensity to ignore this issue entirely, and it is important to ask how it might gain more public attention.

Some suggest that the basic issues could be more readily understood by the public and legislators if OASDI were separated from other government accounts for the purpose of choosing deficit targets. This would presumably attract more attention to the severity of the non-OASDI deficit, which is now being masked by the OASDI annual surplus. If Congress adopted a declining set of targets for the non-OASDI deficit culminating in a small deficit that was constant relative to GNP, the federal government's effect on national saving would rise and then

eventually fall with the OASDI annual surplus.

On the surface, this approach appears highly artificial. It is, of course, the overall deficit that determines the effect of the government on national saving. It should not be that difficult to inform Congress of developments in OASDI and non-OASDI operations and to describe projections of the OASDI and other burdens that will be borne in the twenty-first century. With that information, they should be able to decide on a target for an overall deficit or surplus.

But the federal budget process is already far too complex and time-consuming. Tens of thousands of decisions regarding tax and spending policy have to be made in a limited time, and there is a frequent need to resort to crude rules of thumb to reduce the time spent gathering information and to expedite the decision-making process. The difficulty lies in finding rules of thumb that do not do too much harm to the ration- ality of the result while reducing the complexity of decision making.

If targeting focused on the non-OASDI deficit while placing the operations of the OASDI trust funds completely off budget, it is likely that non-OASDI deficit-reduction efforts would become more vigorous. The other side of the problem is, however, that OASDI would completely escape budget discipline. If payroll tax cuts or benefit increases no longer counted against the official deficit, the political incentives for spending some of the annual surpluses of OASDI would become very powerful. Moreover, there would be no incentive to examine the existing benefit structure in order to see if the burden imposed by OASDI in the future could be eased.

Already, there are proposals to eliminate the OASDI retirement test and to raise benefits for so-called notch babies who unjustifiably believe that they were treated unfairly when indexing was reformed in the late 1970s.[5] Proposals for increased benefits are already being justified by the argument that they have a tiny percentage impact on the annual OASDI surpluses projected for early in the twenty-first century. The restraints on such activities would be eased greatly if OASDI were taken completely off budget. There might also be a move to eliminate the gradual increase in the normal retirement age now scheduled to begin at the start of the twenty-first century.

One would think that the temptation to spend the annual surpluses of OASDI would be restrained by the fact that given the current law, the trust funds are projected to go broke shortly before 2050. However, politicians have notoriously short time horizons, and events projected for the next century often have only trivial effects on their decisions.

Another problem would arise because it is difficult to argue that the OASDI trust funds should be taken off budget while refusing to give off-budget status to other trust funds in the federal government. The civil service trust fund would have a particularly strong claim for off-budget treatment, but other trust funds would also try to achieve off-budget status. If such efforts proved successful, trust funds might be established to finance other government activities.

If one is interested solely in the effect of the federal government on national saving, the key issue raised by the proposal to target only the non-OASDI deficit is whether increased discipline in the non-OASDI operations of government would more than make up for reducing budget discipline in OASDI and in other trust funds successful in obtaining off-budget status. To answer the question requires making a judgment about the strength of the different political incentives created by the proposal, and this judgment must be made with great uncertainty. I believe, however, that there is a very high risk that the end result would be a higher overall government deficit given the extreme political popularity of OASDI. Moreover, it is inherently irrational to target the deficit of only a part of the government. For this reason and the possibility that the goals of the proponents would be thwarted, I oppose taking OASDI completely off budget.

It should be noted that OASDI is already officially off budget, but because the deficit targeted under GRH includes the OASDI annual surplus, OASDI's off-budget status is of little importance. It mainly affects the way that changes in OASDI law must be considered in the budget process. Proposed changes cannot be considered as part of a package of changes also affecting non-OASDI operations; they must be considered separately. This has the effect of making it more difficult to cut OASDI benefits. But this too is unimportant because in the current political atmosphere, it would be virtually impossible to cut OASDI benefits under any set of rules. Moreover, if the political constraints were eased for any reason, the rules could be changed by a majority vote of Congress. Although it is unlikely to make any difference to policy outcomes in the near future, I believe there is some merit in bringing OASDI fully on budget again so that if the opportunity eventually arises, it would be a bit easier to trade off benefits under OASDI against benefits in non-OASDI programs.

Invest the Assets of the OASDI Trust Funds Privately

Currently, the assets of OASDI trust funds must be invested in Treasury securities or securities totally guaranteed by the federal government. Some have suggested that OASDI be allowed to invest its assets privately. The proposal is usually made by those who would like to see OASDI able to earn a higher rate of return so that benefits could be increased or payroll tax rates lowered in the future.

If, however, the entire annual surplus were invested every year in private assets, the effect would be similar to taking OASDI off budget for deficit-targeting purposes. Under current federal accounting practices, which are based on cash flows, purchases of private assets count as outlays; so under these circumstances, the officially measured overall deficit would exactly equal the deficit on non-OASDI operations. But it is important to note that if no other laws were changed, the reform would have no effect on the federal government's impact on national saving. The resources put into private capital markets by OASDI would be exactly matched by increased borrowing to finance non-

OASDI operations. The total amount of saving and investment would not change, although the composition of investment might change to the extent that OASDI decision makers choose different investments than would have been made by private investors.[6]

The OASDI annual surpluses would no longer be masking the non-OASDI deficit, and that might create more discipline in that part of government, but discipline might erode in OASDI and in other areas of government acquiring the same status. However, the proposal should not be judged on these grounds.

The more important issue is whether the government should assume the important role in private capital markets implied by this proposal. If investments were made to maximize risk-adjusted profits, there would be little to worry about, but there might be a temptation to use OASDI investment policy to achieve social goals. This would reduce the ability of OASDI to increase its rate of return and would provide another opportunity for legislators to achieve social goals without the costs being apparent in the budget. Because of this danger, I do not believe that this reform is desirable.

Allow Private Pensions to Substitute for Social Security

An interesting proposal by the Morgan Guaranty Trust Company would allow individuals to divert up to, say, 2 percentage points of their payroll tax liability to a private pension fund. This would hold down the growth in the OASDI trust fund, thus reducing the temptation to spend it, and would have the effect of privately investing a portion of currently scheduled payroll taxes. The private investments would be under private control, thus avoiding the disadvantages of having private investment controlled by public officials. Private investors would,however, have to bear the risk of adverse outcomes. The allowable diversion of payroll tax revenues would be reviewed periodically and adjusted depending on the path of the trust fund balance and the number of individuals who chose this option.

This partial privatization of public pensions has considerable appeal, but it also has some important disadvantages. Although the plan would have considerable appeal for almost all younger workers, it would have special appeal to higher-income workers whose rate of return from Social Security is much lower than that accruing to lower-income workers. (Their rate of return on payroll contributions is likely to be lower than the average rate of return on private pensions.) Moreover, for lower-income workers, the amounts involved would be quite small; and to them, it might not be worth the bother. (An average worker would today be able to divert less than $400 per year.)

Consequently, the plan would mainly be advantageous to higher-income and younger workers, and this might be perceived as unfair. Moreover, higher-income workers play an important role in subsidizing the system in the long run. As more of them opted out relative to low-income workers, the eventual depletion of the trust fund could be accelerated to the point that it would not be feasible to continue the plan through a high proportion of the working life of today's younger workers. The plan would also have significant administrative costs and would require a major education program to inform people about the wisdom of opting for the private investment of their contribution.

Reduce the OASDI Annual Surplus

Because of the danger that politicians will not be able to resist spending the OASDI surplus, a radically different approach to the problem would be to prevent the surplus from burgeoning in the first place. This could be done by eliminating the payroll tax increase scheduled for 1990 and reversing a portion of the tax increase that went into effect in 1988.

Of course, if that were all that was done, the overall government deficit would rise and national savings would fall. Therefore, to be sensible, the payroll tax cut would have to be combined with an equivalent decrease in non-OASDI spending or an increase in some other taxes, very probably personal and corporate income taxes.

In the longer run, if a huge accumulated surplus is not allowed to develop in the trust fund, there would be more of an incentive to reexamine the generosity of Social Security benefits as the surge of benefits after 2005 come closer. If that resulted in some slowing in their real growth, the burden imposed on future workers would obviously be lowered. If the present value of the promises made to the elderly could be reduced somewhat, the need to increase national savings currently would be diminished slightly, but it would still be very important given that any politically conceivable benefit reduction is bound to be modest.

22

If the surplus in OASDI is not allowed to grow, the deficit targets used in the budget process could continue to be expressed including the OASDI trust fund. Other government trust funds would then have no excuse for escaping budget discipline.

The reduction in the payroll tax appeals to those who argue that the current overall tax system is insufficiently progressive. They would argue further that even if national savings could be increased in the long run by stating deficit targets exclusive of OASDI, it is not a good way of accomplishing that end. Essentially, it implies heavy reliance on the payroll tax to raise national savings, and that is not fair because the payroll tax is regressive at high income levels. Of course, fairness is in the eye of the beholder, and some would argue that the current tax system as a whole already redistributes too much income.

The reduced reliance on payroll taxes implied by this option has another potential disadvantage. Wage taxes tend to resemble closely consumption taxes once all the economic effects are worked out. Moving the tax system toward greater reliance on income taxes would therefore have a slight negative effect on private savings. But there are alternative ways of encouraging private savings, and this argument may not have much merit.

It should be noted that the regressive nature of the payroll tax is often overstated. Indeed, it is sometimes called the most regressive tax in our system. That is an exaggeration. Excise taxes are much more regressive. Measured relative

to family income, the payroll tax is, in fact, quite progressive at the bottom of the income scale. Low-income individuals are often in that state because they are retired or unable to find suitable work because of physical problems or lack of skills. Thus, they pay little payroll tax relative to their income, which consists largely of transfer payments. For full-time workers, the payroll tax is roughly proportional up to the maximum wage base, which is $48,000 in 1989. Even slightly above that amount, the tax is close to proportional over a wide range since in many families, total income only exceeds the maximum wage base because more than one family member is working. It is only at high wage levels that the tax becomes significantly regressive. Chart 3 illustrates the payroll tax burden by different family income categories.

It remains true, however, that the payroll tax viewed in isolation is much less progressive than the personal income tax. But the OASDI benefit and tax system viewed as a whole is progressive in the sense that those with relatively low covered wages over a lifetime earn higher benefits relative to taxes paid than those with higher lifetime covered wages.

Reducing the Future Burden Imposed by OASDI and HI

A reduction in the value of the benefits provided by OASDI and HI would seem, at first sight, to reduce the standard of living of future retirees while lowering the burden on future workers. However, the way in which the burden is spread over the generations will depend crucially on the private response to reduced

CHART 3

PAYROLL TAX BURDEN BY DECILES, 1988

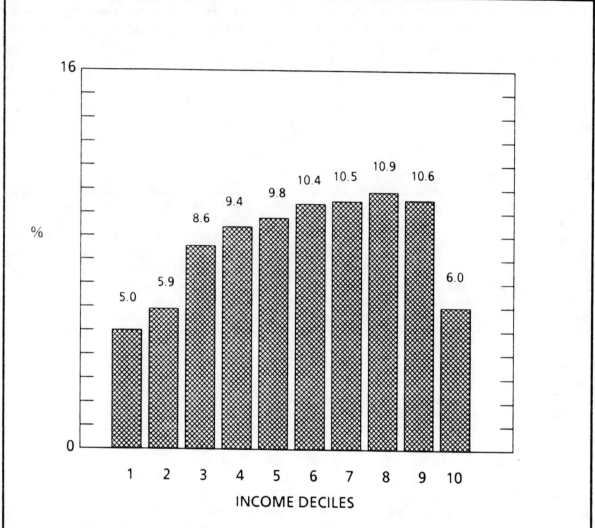

NOTE: Average family income by decile are as follows: first, $3,676; second, $8,043; third, $12,874; fourth, $17,967; fifth, $23,324; sixth $29,333; seventh, $36,174; eighth, $45,045; ninth, $58,103; tenth, $128,631. The computations assume that the corporate tax burdens only capital income.

Source: Congressional Budget Office, <u>The Changing Distribution of Federal Taxes: 1975-1990,</u> (Washington D.C. : U.S. Government Printing Office, October 1987). pp. 39 and 47.

24

benefits in the future. If future public benefits are lowered, workers may decide to replace a part or all of the lost benefits by increasing saving currently. Future workers may also decide to transfer more income to their parents privately if benefits are lowered. The exact effect on future workers is unclear, but it is more likely to be positive than negative. To the extent that current workers increase private saving to make up for the loss in future public benefits, the productivity and wages of future workers would be increased and the burden of payroll taxes and private transfers to the elderly would be eased. Moreover, it seems unlikely that private transfers would entirely make up for the loss in public benefits.

There are many options for lowering OASDI benefits, but none of these are likely to be very popular politically. Certainly, it is hard to contemplate cuts that would significantly reduce the benefits of current retirees or cuts for those retiring in the near future. One exception to this rule may be the option to tax Social Security benefits as though they were private pensions. That would involve allowing some credit for the portion of benefits financed by the worker's share of the payroll tax, since it is not deductible against taxable income. Today, the credit would amount to at most about 15 percent of benefits. In other words, 85 percent of benefits would be subject to taxation compared with the 50 percent now taxable for more affluent retirees. Very poor elderly would not be affected because they do not pay income taxes, and those with modest incomes would be affected very little.

In my judgment, the only other benefit reductions worth contempla-

ting are those that would occur far enough in the future to give current workers adequate time to increase private pensions by saving more on their own or through their employers. Many might choose not to take advantage of the opportunity to add to private pensions, but they must be given the chance.

One approach to the problem would be to increase the normal retirement age to a greater extent and somewhat faster than envisioned in current law.

Life expectancy at age 65 has been rising significantly. In 1970, it was 15 years. By 1985, it had risen to 16.7 years, and it is expected to continue to rise in the future. For a given benefit structure, that implies that the expected present value of benefits is continually rising. In that sense, the generosity of the system is constantly improving given current law.

Current law provides full benefits at age 65 for workers and spouses who reach age 62 before 2000. For cohorts reaching age 62 in 2000 and later, the normal retirement age is increased by two months per year until it reaches 66 in 2009 for those reaching 62 in 2005. It is held at 66 for those who attain that age in the period from 2010 through 2020. It is then again raised by two months per year until it reaches 67 in 2027.

It would seem reasonable to eliminate the pause in retirement age increases in the 2010-to-2020 period and to continually raise the age at which full benefits are paid by two months per year until it reaches 70 in 2037.

This pattern has some appealing attributes. It would give

current workers plenty of time to adjust. It would not affect anyone reaching age 62 before 2006. Moreover, compared with current law, the normal retirement age would be increasing about the same time that the ratio of the retired to the working population will be rising rapidly.

Individuals could still be allowed to retire at age 62, but they would have to accept actuarially reduced benefits. An increase in the retirement age, therefore, has similar effects to reducing the replacement rate at every age by altering the formula that determines initial benefits.

The rapid rise in annual OASDI surpluses over the next thirty years will make it difficult to induce Congress to consider a further increase in the retirement age and could possibly cause it to cancel the increase contained in current law. It would therefore be desirable to encourage such a change by allowing an immediate cut in the payroll tax rate in order to put OASDI on an explicit pay-as-you-go basis. The goal of keeping the trust fund balance equivalent to 100 percent of outlays could be established.

If OASDI payroll taxes are cut, it is essential that equivalent spending cuts occur in the non-OASDI budget or that other taxes be increased by the amount that payroll tax revenues are decreased. Otherwise, an already serious deficit problem would deteriorate further. Admittedly, this greatly reduces the political appeal of this option, but it is the only circumstance in which payroll taxes should be cut.

The easiest tax substitution might involve increasing HI taxes by a portion of the OASDI tax cut.

This would have the effect of moving the HI systems toward actuarial balance. Otherwise, it will be bankrupt early in the twenty-first century. In the interim, large surpluses would temporarily accumulate in the HI trust fund, but there should be little temptation to spend them because the problems of financing HI benefits in the long run are apparent and much more immediate than the long-run problems facing OASDI.

Because an increase in the normal retirement age begins to ease the OASDI burden after 2010, shortly before the accumulated assets of the trust funds peak relative to GNP under current law, it reduces the extent to which the employer-payroll tax of 12.4 percent, now scheduled after 1989, would have to be increased in the very long run in order to achieve actuarial balance. Indeed, it allows the adoption of a pay-as-you-go approach without resorting to a very rapid increase in payroll tax rates after 2005 required by a pay-as-you-go system given the normal retirement age implied by current law.

Table 3 compares the currently scheduled payroll tax rates with those required by a pay-as-you-go approach given the current normal retirement age and with those required if the retirement age is increased as I have described. The payroll tax rate increase now scheduled for 1990 would not be necessary, and in fact, the rate could be cut a bit. The rates are provided for illustrative purposes only. They are based on the IIB assumptions, and to the degree that those assumptions prove inaccurate, rates would have to be adjusted from time to time. For this reason, it would probably be preferable not to enact the rate cuts beyond 1994, so that taxpayers will not be disappointed

Table 3

OASDI Employer-Employee Payroll Rates Under Different Options

Year	Present Law	Pay as You Go	
		Current - Law Retirement Age	Delayed Retirement Age
1988-1989	12.12 %	12.12 %	12.12 %
1990-1994	12.40	11.40	11.40
1995-2009	12.40	10.20	10.20
2010-2014	12.40	10.20	10.10
2015-2019	12.40	12.00	11.70
2020-2024	12.40	13.60	12.40
2025-2048	12.40	15.20	12.80
2049 +	12.40	15.40	13.00

NOTE: The author would like to thank Robert J. Myers for his assistance in developing this table. The rates shown do not include the tax rate for the HI portion of Medicare.

if economic or demographic developments do not allow further rate reductions.

If OASDI is put on a pay-as-you-go system, the annual surpluses implied by current law will be greatly decreased and the temptation to increase the generosity of benefits will be greatly reduced. It is important, however, to put OASDI completely on budget so that there is a stronger incentive to go through with the increase in the retirement age once it is established. Moreover, the generosity of benefits should be continually reexamined. Very minor changes in Social Security benefits can save as much as some very painful changes in smaller programs. There will be little incentive to consider such reforms if OASDI is completely off budget.

I noted earlier that Medicare will greatly increase the burden facing future workers if current law is not changed. There are numerous approaches to easing the future Medicare burden, by reducing either benefits or the fees paid to health care providers. Such options have been analyzed elsewhere and will not be discussed here.

However, if the OASDI normal retirement age is increased, it is important to consider a comparable increase in the age at which people become eligible for Medicare. Under current law, the eligibility age for Medicare will remain at 65 when the normal retirement age under OASDI begins to rise in the early twenty-first century. Considerable savings would be possible if the eligibility age for Medicare were increased along with the increase recommended for OASDI. The savings would not, however, be proportional to the

reduction in the eligible population because the younger elderly are much cheaper to serve than those who are older.

If the normal retirement age is raised more quickly and to a greater extent than implied by current law, it is natural to consider an increase in the lower-bound retirement age of 62 as well. This would not result in long-run OASDI savings because those opting for earlier retirement must accept actuarially reduced benefits. The main reason for increasing the lower-bound age would be to create stronger disincentives for early retirement so that the nation could benefit from a larger labor force. The quantitative impact of this option on the size of the labor force deserves further study.

CONCLUSIONS

This analysis rejects the recommendations of those who would like to put OASDI completely off budget for deficit-targeting purposes. Although it is true that putting OASDI completely off budget would draw more attention to the non-OASDI deficit and might result in more vigorous deficit-reducing actions in the non-OASDI operations of government, it would remove budget discipline from OASDI and could result in an increase in OASDI benefits. In addition, other trust funds might exploit the precedent and thereby escape budget discipline. It is not clear that the overall deficit would be improved, and there is a substantial risk that it would be worsened.

There is no reason why OASDI should be exempted from the budget discipline facing the rest of government. It is true that there is a moral contract not to change OASDI benefits abruptly, but the system should be continually scrutinized to identify possible options for gradual long-term savings. Moreover, it is the overall government deficit that indicates its effect on national saving and it is therefore the overall deficit that should be targeted. It can be legitimately argued that a longer time horizon should be used in developing a national saving policy and that more attention should be paid to the long-run composition of spending and revenues, but removing OASDI from the budget does not significantly enhance that process.

The option for reducing the future burden of OASDI favored here is to increase the normal retirement age more rapidly and to a greater extent than scheduled in current law. The system could then be put on a pay-as-you-go basis to remove any temptation to spend the large annual surpluses expected through 2030 given currently scheduled payroll tax rates. The payroll tax increases eventually necessitated by a pay-as-you-go system could be significantly reduced if the normal retirement age is increased. The future burden imposed by Medicare could be reduced by increasing the eligibility age for that program along with the normal retirement age.

The reduced burden on future generations implied by these options does not greatly reduce the need to increase national saving currently. Saving is extraordinarily low by past standards and so must be considered too low even if demographic trends did not imply a future rise in the ratio of the retired to the working population.

The need for greater national saving implies that the immediate reduction in payroll taxes made possible by a pay-as-you-go approach would have to be compensated for by spending cuts or tax increases in non-OASDI operations so that the overall deficit would not be increased. If this proves impossible politically, I would not favor a pay-as-you-go approach.

More generally, I have no illusions about the political difficulty of implementing my recommendations. It will be extremely difficult to persuade Congress to raise the normal retirement age given the large annual surpluses expected under current law. Moreover, the change has to be made quickly in order to give people time to adjust. It will also be difficult to get compensating tax increases or spending reductions elsewhere if payroll tax rates are reduced under a pay-as-you-go approach and then to get the further spending cuts or tax increases necessary to increase national saving above current levels. It is not clear, however, that it would be that much easier to get non-OASDI spending cuts or tax increases if the non-OASDI deficit is targeted. The American people are currently extremely hostile to any tax increases or program cuts.

But somehow Americans must be persuaded that if we continue with current policy, we are treating future generations very badly relative to how our predecessors treated us. If we do not act courageously, the inevitable result will be lower future living standards than would otherwise be possible and a nation that will become relatively weaker as a world power.

ENDNOTES

[1] Alicia H. Munnell and Lynn E. Blais, "Do We Want Large Social Security Surpluses?" New England Economic Review (Boston, MA: Federal Reserve Bank of Boston, September-October 1984), pp. 5-21.

[2] For a summary of the literature, see Rudolph G. Penner, "Economic Growth," in Challenge to Leadership, ed. Isabel Sawhill (Washington, D.C.: Urban Institute, 1988), pp. 67-100.

[3] Edward M. Gramlich, "How Bad Are the Large Deficits?" in Federal Budget Policy in 1980, ed. Gregory B. Mills and John L. Palmer (Washington, D.C.: The Urban Institute Press, 1984), pp. 52-59; and Penner, "Economic Growth."

[4] Henry J. Aaron, Barry P. Bosworth, and Gary Burtless, Can America Afford to Grow Old? (Washington, D.C.: The Brookings Institution, 1988).

[5] For an excellent discussion of the notch problem, see Robert J. Myers, Gary Burtless, Suzanne B. Dilk, and James W. Kelley, The Social Security Benefit Notch: A Study (Washington, D.C.: National Academy of Social Insurance, November 1988).

[6] This paragraph ignores the fact that the earnings on private investment would probably exceed the increased interest paid or increased Treasury borrowing. As a result, the budget deficit would fall a little and national saving might rise by a small amount.

[7] See Congressional Budget Office, Reducing the Deficit: Spending and Revenue Options (Washington, D.C.: U.S. Government Printing Office, March 1988), Part 4.

Committee for Economic Development
477 Madison Avenue
New York, New York 10022